An Exploration of M.A.R.S.

Poems Inspired by the Art of Marco Antonio Rosales Shaw

Published by Maria Rosales

Poems by :

Suzanne Bruce

Susan Condeff

Deborah Fruchey

William Landis

Indigo Moor

Stan Morner

Maria Rosales

Sherry Sheehan

Deborah Silverman

Sandra Lee Stillwell

This book was born after an unforgettable reading of these poems alongside the paintings which inspired them, in the Campbell Theatre in Martinez, California, October 25th, 2014. Thank you to all the poets who played in the sandbox of ekphrasis with Marco.

Maria Rosales

Contents

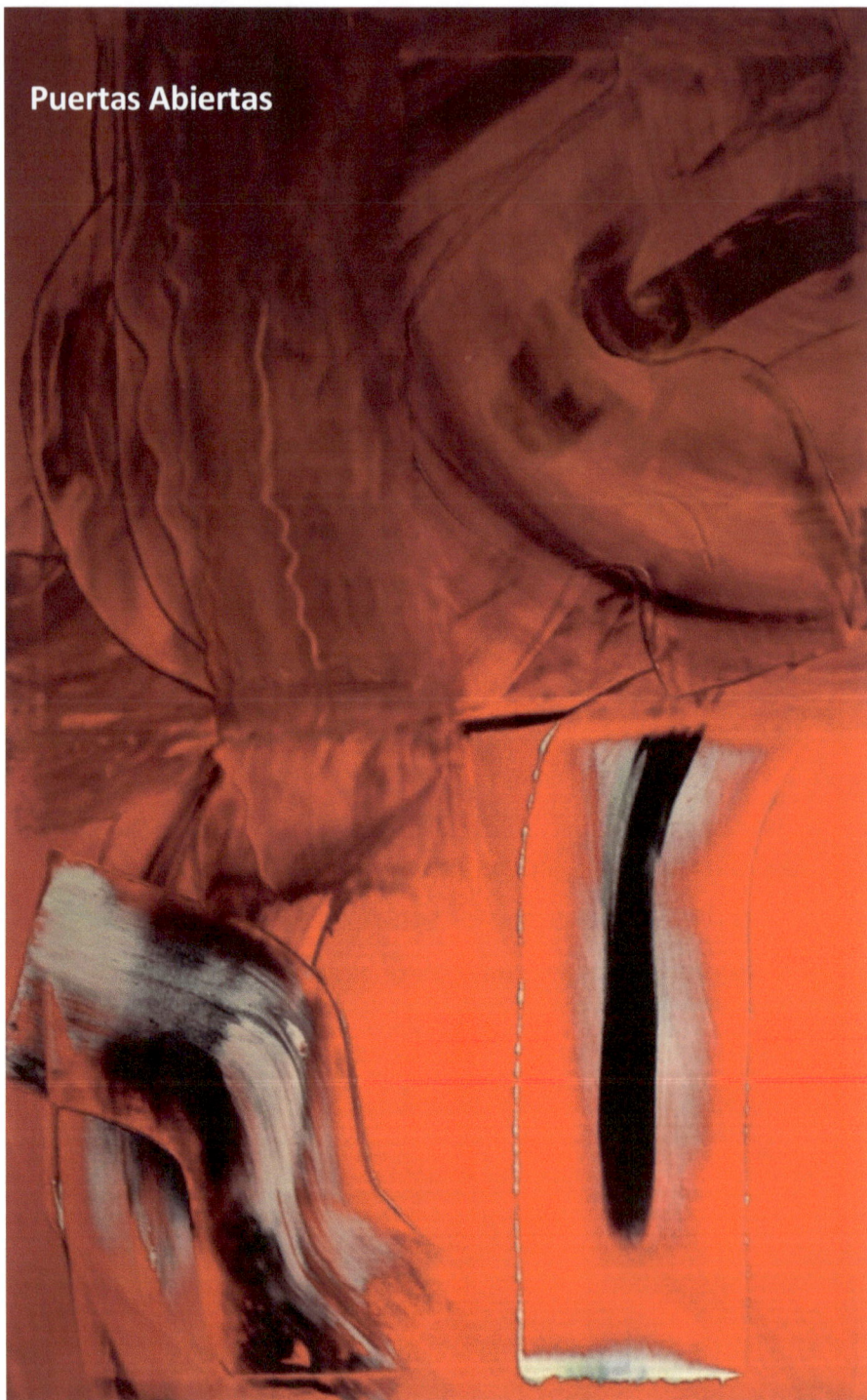

Puertas Abiertas

PUERTAS ABIERTAS
After the painting *Puertas Abiertas* by Marco Rosales Shaw
by Indigo Moor

Understanding
        the hubris inherent
in Dorian Gray's
psyche, you paint
        flesh with flesh,
cast heart pulp
down as if it were *Toro Bravo.*

Slowly pump
varying shades,
        red across four
chambers of canvas.
        Always

mindful of the shaman's
warning: *Never*
        sell this original.

In all its frangibility
enfolding, brittle
                synthesis
        of blood and fervor
we are reminded:
this is your chest split-
                ripe, the heart
        still beating
like a blacksmith's forge.

Royal chestnut
        bleeds into dark
Venetian
        top to bottom
        as your strokes
contract and relax

3

diastole
        & systole, piston
work of your passion.

Through your left
        and right atriums,
        thick crimson ripples,
raised in relief,
hold court with
an orange Cordoban hat,
throbbing like
an autumn sun.

Below, calming fervor
is woven into ventricles:
        flamenco boots
in blurred motion.

A noose-thin tie
laid flat, restrains
        a wan
                river cascading.

And all the while
the canvas tinged
        with undulating waves

as if
(in afterthought) you
offer up your trackwork
        of nerves in sacrifice,
pulsing
        with cryptic lightning.

Previously published in *Through the Stonecutter's Window*, winner of
Northwestern University Press's *Cave Canem* prize.

THRESHOLDS

After the painting *Puertas Abiertas* by Marco Rosales Shaw

by Deborah Fruchey

Any doorway
Secretly opens
Galaxies.

Loiterers will be persecuted.

Step lively,
Now.

Labyrinth

ORGANIC ALCHEMY

After the painting *Labyrinth* by Marco Rosales Shaw

by Stan Morner

Glimpse test tube samples of yin and yang
In their ever present binary circulation.
Helix high molecules waft skyward,
Follow discrete flight plans.
Grasp the spew of living stew
Before it squirms through the flue
Of empty-headed microscope
Cognition.

Catch the Chinese Dragon as it writhes,
Fiber fingers of feeling sliding through
The froth filled mane of alchemy's Ancient Lion.
Find fertility, freshness, the Green Tara.

Know the Krishna fibers of bent arrows.
Do not be distracted by detachment.
Make solitude solid and strong
Even in the loneliness of questing
Erections and blue-hot lightning.

Twelve strands seek to contain the sea,
Cone-like heads bumping the bottom
Where a universe of transfiguration
Stands with feet in soiled sand.
All tubes are swallowed and nurtured
By an ocean of linear wonder
Deep and wild in their own
wombs.

Somewhere in Baja

SOMEWHERE IN BAJA
After the painting *Somewhere in Baja* by Marco Rosales Shaw
by Sherry Sheehan

The planet we ride, a body in space,
is aswirl in clouds and water –
emotions that erode its shores
of reason and resistance.

I, a rider, look for the demarcations
that maps give to identify
these separate realms.

Occasionally boundaries shift
and blur, and what was one thing
becomes another. I might
perceive the blue as sky, not ocean.

I might see that tanned green
as a hillside in front of me,
not land viewed by a mapmaker,
in control on paper.

Any bird would know,
but I feel so much slosh
in my compass that I cannot
always differentiate

between a profiled cliff
up ahead and land meeting sea
in a blue-green collision below.

An avian in flight feels direction.
It needs no maps, markers,
or global positioning system.
It's never awash in being lost

as I am – eyes searching,
recognizing nothing, nerves pecked
by a thousand beaks, a cliff
appearing where no cliff should be

JUST IN TIME TO SEE FOUR PAINTINGS

The Crow, The Sagging House, Death With One Breast, & Somewhere In Baja
After the painting *Somewhere in Baja* by Marco Rosales Shaw
by William Landis

the crow remembers returning to the arc
    with mud on his feet   loud and proud
in his own crow way   as if none of us
    has a bigger answer and we don't

the wood house is sagging   has given up arguing
    with sassy white grasses brushing its thighs
the families sliding into emptiness
    looking perhaps for a witness to history
they ask the crow about futility

the crow and the house reminisce at night
    with a raw headless torso in a cowboy hat
Death with her one perfect breast exposed
    the rest of her is graffiti on a fence
where the other breast once was

but far from here somewhere in Baja
    the land is wider and hotter
without the meaningless things called fences
    as for borders and privacy issues
the barking dogs never sleep

everyone knows somewhere in Baja
    that splendor cannot be boxed in   that sunsets
find whoever stands in the light
    that thirst blesses the one who drinks
and love is natural as firewood

somewhere in Baja you begin to accept it
    paved roads and cell phones lose their appeal
and sleep is the magic of waking up whole
    the magic of tasting the very first bite
of every precious day

SOMEWHERE IN BAJA
After the painting *Somewhere in Baja* by Marco Rosales Shaw
by Susan Condeff

I left myself for dead
Created a fire of sadness
Buried your memory in shadowy blue caves
My pulse stopped for you
Heart crystallized
Became sand
I fell into pieces of my own beach
Marooned
Alone
Little deaths are necessary and stunning

Thank God for warmth and sun
Time and prayer

I bathed in self, hope and warm indigo
Emerged clean, refreshed

Swam in waves of wish and new
Befriended fish and faith
Found treasure in myself

Somewhere in Baja

I left myself for dead
And walked away

The Dance

THE DANCE
After the painting *The Dance* by Marco Rosales Shaw
by William Landis

if my feet can find the wind I will dance
I will stand on my head and speak with my feet

a wind full of fury and shredded lettuce and prayers
how it brings a friend when you least expect it

how it brings each seasons and tells me how small I am
how it twists into grief when youngsters die

how it gentles the miracle of death itself
the perfection of it   the same—ever the same surprise

the way wind hollows out a whistle or a song
in the ramparts of a tree

should my face find rain doing a jig
look for benevolence in the afternoon

if my heart can locate dandelions dancing
I will make wine that gentles the elders to their feet

when my heart deciphers whispers in the wind
I will write and paint the sorrow inside laughter

if I write and paint the sorrow inside laughter
the wind will say I have danced

NACHTMUSIK
After the painting *The Dance* by Marco Rosales Shaw
by Stan Morner

The blind dancing girl speaks:
"Motion wills what it will will,
Swells what wells in the inner cave,
Just as day is night
And the bird's unseen song
Starlights a blue marble sky
Where inverted dancers live and die."

The sage touches her eyes:
"Your heart is a silver moon
Sweeping the obsidian dance floor
Of your silent soul's keen sight.
Hard scrabble facts are lover lost
In the dervish whirl of your sublimations
That entangle virgins and sages tonight."

She knows without seeing.
He sees without knowing.
Together they invent a dance
Of light and darkness
To the blue and silver night music.

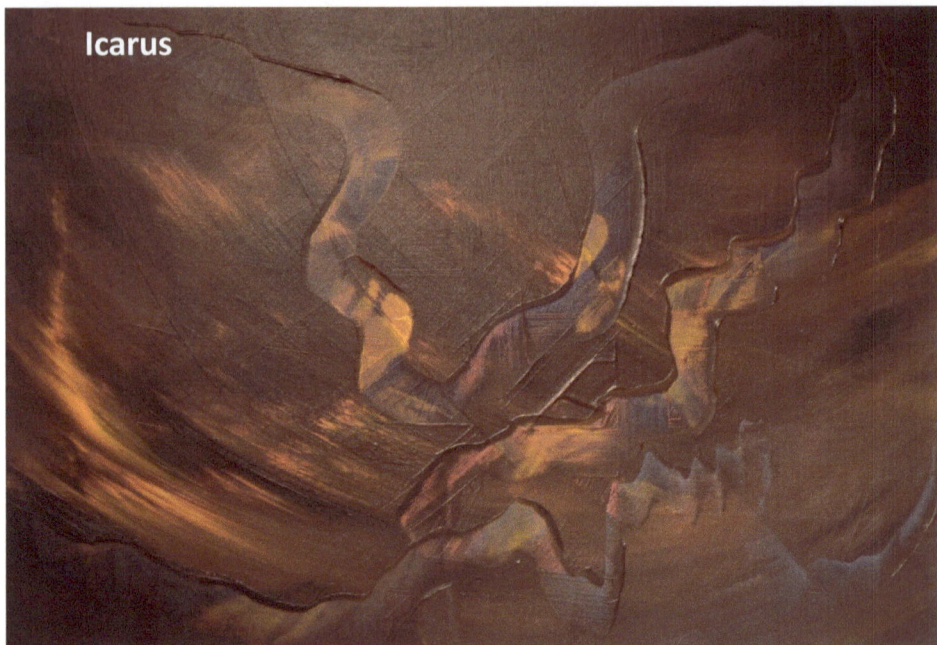

Icarus

THE ICARUS GENE
After the painting *Icarus* by Marco Rosales Shaw
by Deborah Fruchey

Animals still recall his fall.
Flying fish scuttle and whir
Only a cautious inch or two
above the waves.
Monkeys stick to treetops; most
stick to the ground.
Even birds, the first transgressors,
don't aim for the sun itself.
Moths are a grim exception
goslings whisper of.

But humans remember best the flight,
and build steel pterodactyls,
riding in the bellies,
or invent new lights that do not burn.
The feathered shake their heads.
It's in their genes, say geese.
They cannot help it.

It is rumored
that the missing link
lies decomposing in Tibet
a human skeleton
with broad up-arching wings
and tiny, broken feet.
The humans know
it is their fate to fall
but only
from the greatest height they can.

FLIGHT
After the painting *Icarus* by Marco Rosales Shaw
by Suzanne Bruce

No longer willing to tolerate
confining walls, you looked up,
performed what others

couldn't even imagine,
freedom embroidered through flight.
Feathers tethered to wings of wax,

you flitted and flew like uncaptured glee,
your eyes, fanatical, seduced
by goldness of fun, frivolity.

Although warned of heat from sun,
dampness of the sea,
euphoria corroded safety's touch.

What were your thoughts
as silky winds polished your wet wings,
as the elixir you enjoyed from open sky

intoxicated you,
as you were drawn to the light
that caused your demise?

Like mortals that need to know
there is a time when life is everything,
then nothing,

shall we genuflect that cathedral presence
where your shadow was larger than yourself?
Did your heart still strive to survive,

as you fell
into an unforgiving sea
of purple death?

CONTACT
After the painting *Icarus* by Marco Rosales Shaw
by Stan Morner

feet splayed in an off balance dive
almost head first but maybe flat
the time for form expired as the fall started
all those dreams of arabesques and freedom
nothing now but waiting for the final splat

Yet he's as flashy as a sentient astroid
dropping out of the sky this Icarus
the boy remembers flight as pure structure
movement accompanied by clouds of sound
the carefully contained joy of Respighi's birds
the embrace of Debussy's blue tone ride
the agony of Messiaen's synesthesia
ripping off his wings like a crust of paint flakes
he's down to Scriabin's poem of ecstasy and fire
the moment he realizes those prophecies
of revelation and the fatalism of nemesis
apply to his spinning and grasping form

Marco stops Icarus here
as he joins the whole herd of heroes
who held hubris in tight fists
just before the moment of contact

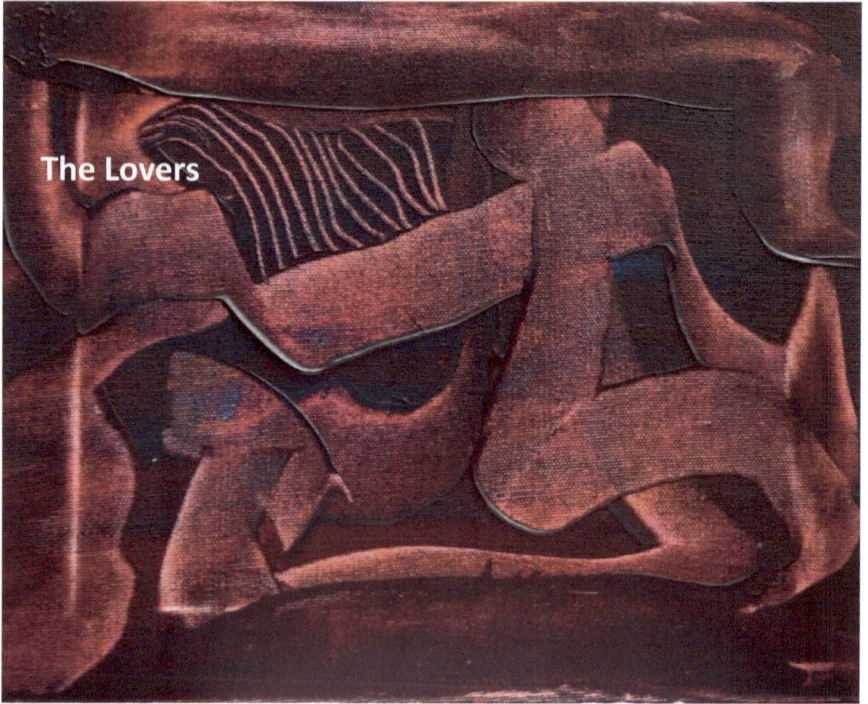

The Lovers

THE LOVERS
After the painting *The Lovers* by Marco Rosales Shaw
by Sherry Sheehan

He drew them bendable
and sinewy as first love,

put them underground
in a warm cave,

etched their shapes
with raspberry ink

into a slab of stone
the color of dark chocolate,

making art from the night
of their first encounter

so that years later
they would remember

what she couldn't recall
without blushing.

Sueño en el Tropico

DREAM OF THE TROPICS
After the painting *Sueño en el Tropico* by Marco Rosales Shaw
by Sherry Sheehan

"Boats—he's had one since boyhood," says Mom while taking my small self to elementary school. "He loves the ocean. When he didn't show up for dinner, your grandmother told me that she assumed he'd sailed to another island and forgotten to come home." Navigating by the stars, Dad too often roams from one island to another. As long as I can remember, he's spent most weekends on his boat with his fishing buddies who don't mind smelly, rough bunk beds. Mom's way to experience a nautical adventure is by immersing herself in the Raoul Dufy prints she's framed and hung on our walls. Dufy's racing sailboats are shot through with colors that match the fabrics she feeds to her Singer and the gowns she models each week in Waikiki. I don't dream of the tropics—I waken daily in them, fantasizing a version where jungles of color merge and stay blended, where forms cohere, where we three are together, and families never fracture.

A DREAM OF THE TROPICS
After the Painting *Sueño en el Tropico* by Marco Rosales Shaw
by Sandra Lee Stillwell

Delicate wind, wish warm
gathers aqua from salty sea vapors
and mist rising from monsoons passing
then wraps itself around my body
bright as a scarf of sun warmed silk.

Wind borrowing a tinge of apricot
from wide-brimmed hibiscus
lush green from the jungle's canopy,
a bit of red violet from native orchids
and starlit midnight blue stolen
from the sweet passion of night
teases a dreamy morning from sultry to sweet.

Wind wearing the perfume of the tropics
inspiring dreams of brown- skinned people
wearing white embroidered
with the vivid colors of their lives
people with dark eyes that dance with life,
laughter and love.

Wind inspiring dreams of colorful sails on indigo water,
white sand and unfamiliar comfort.
I awake alone in Northern California
to the sound of hail hammering down on the roof,
a wind that has never known warmth.

Between flannel sheets,
I have indulged in a little vacation
warmed my toes in somebody else's sand,
waking now, not only to hail, but the heady fragrance of orchids.

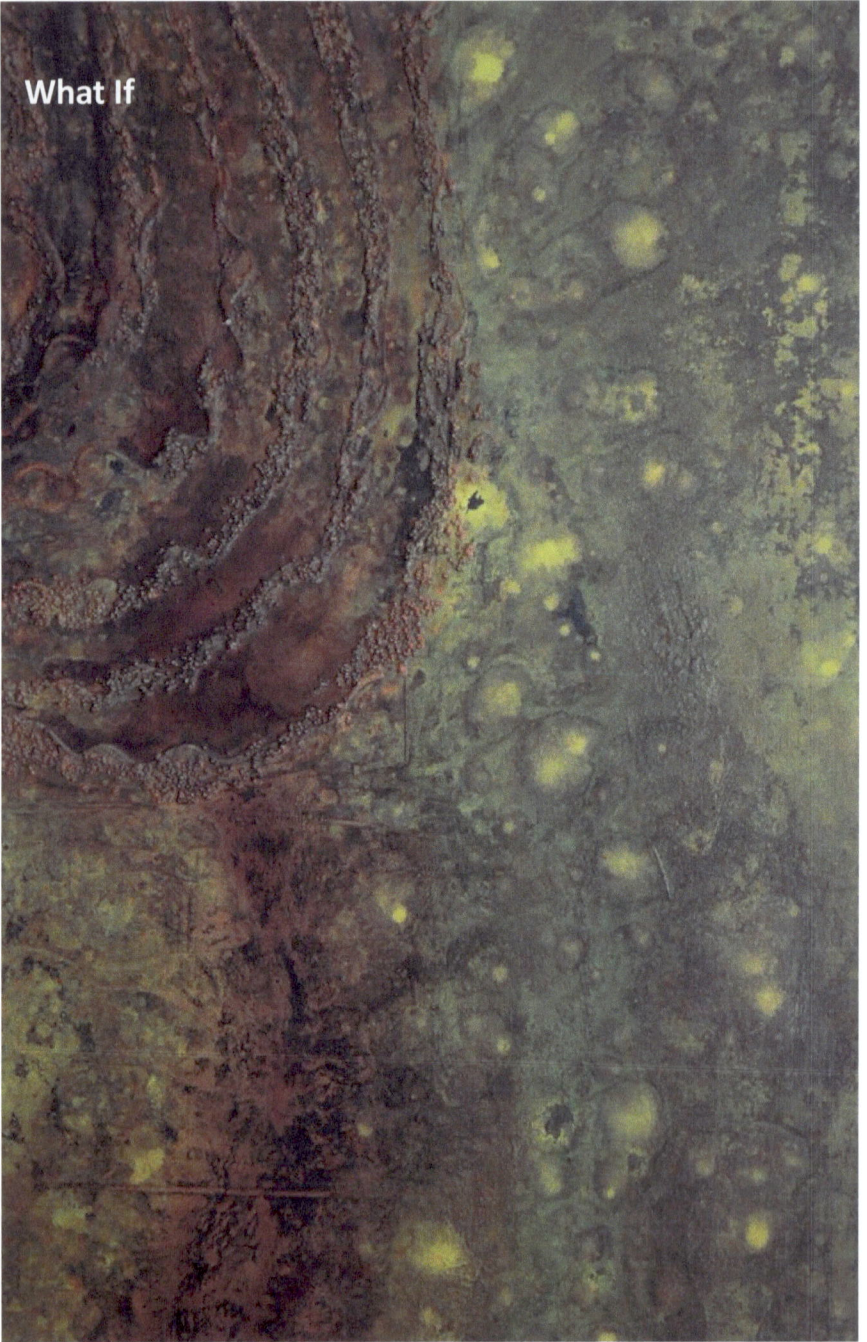

What If

WHAT IF
After the painting *What If* by Marco Rosales Shaw
By Stan Morner

"These chains of events all indeed happen, simultaneously. For in this world, time has three dimensions, like space. Just as an object may move in three perpendicular directions, corresponding to horizontal, vertical, and longitudinal, so an object may participate in three perpendicular futures."

Alan Lightman, *Einstein's Dreams* (Pantheon Books: New York, 1993) pp. 21-22

her sexuality
was a beaded mountain of centuries
his psyche
unable to untangle and dangle
the skylight of her blended hills
she screamed and the fuse of her form
faded into brown earth central
he spewed out baby galaxies
of yellow stars that became
pimples of memory

he led off
with a green sky of crackled dreams
defying agreed upon notions of reality
her slumping arcs of burnt umber desire drifted
into odd circles of cucumber growth
defying agreed upon notions of reality
and left birds disguised as the love planet
in copper metal and medals in his heart

hoped for harmony
honed home after many missed cycles
the eyes of subdued suns
held a singular sky quivering
with speckled rivers, pebbles and a green horizon
and man and woman
clung to the double sweetness where they could stay
defying all notions of agreed upon reality

31

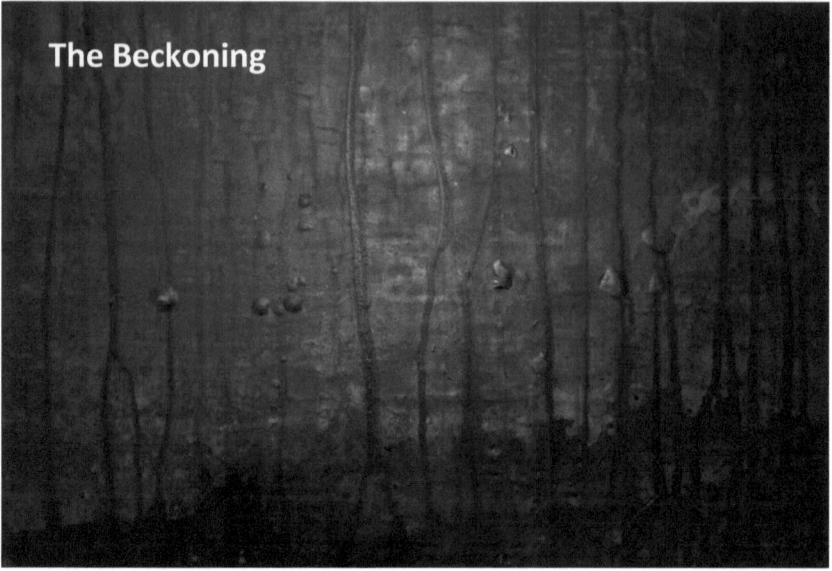

The Beckoning

MARCO'S TREES
After the painting *The Beckoning* by Marco Rosales Shaw
by William Landis

to see a line of trees

    a regiment at attention

soldiering on (yet in place like a river)

    contradicting the hovering light

to see   to not see

    we   also imbedded in a life

brushing our hope against the belly of the sky

    this bowl of light we drink from

trying to navigate a life

    the what of it   the white-out descending

the liquid air the wet thick sky

    the far-reaching immediacy slapping my face

to be beckoned into a painting

    to find yourself wandering inside its questioning

is to finger the footprints of philosophers

    is to ponder the laughter of leaves

is to pin the question mark suspended in light

   with the mark of exclamation

to wander in wonder

   inside a fuzzy delight

BEHIND IT ALL
After the painting *The Beckoning* by Marco Rosales Shaw
by Deborah Silverman

beyond my easeful everyday

blurring earth's glories

other stories

worlds afar through war-scarred eyes

and here, cloaked in urbanity

cries of forgotten humanity

behind a façade of democracy

moans of injustice, lavish lies

as stock markets rise

the shadow of new high

rises fall and beneath it all

the flow of tears, the muted call

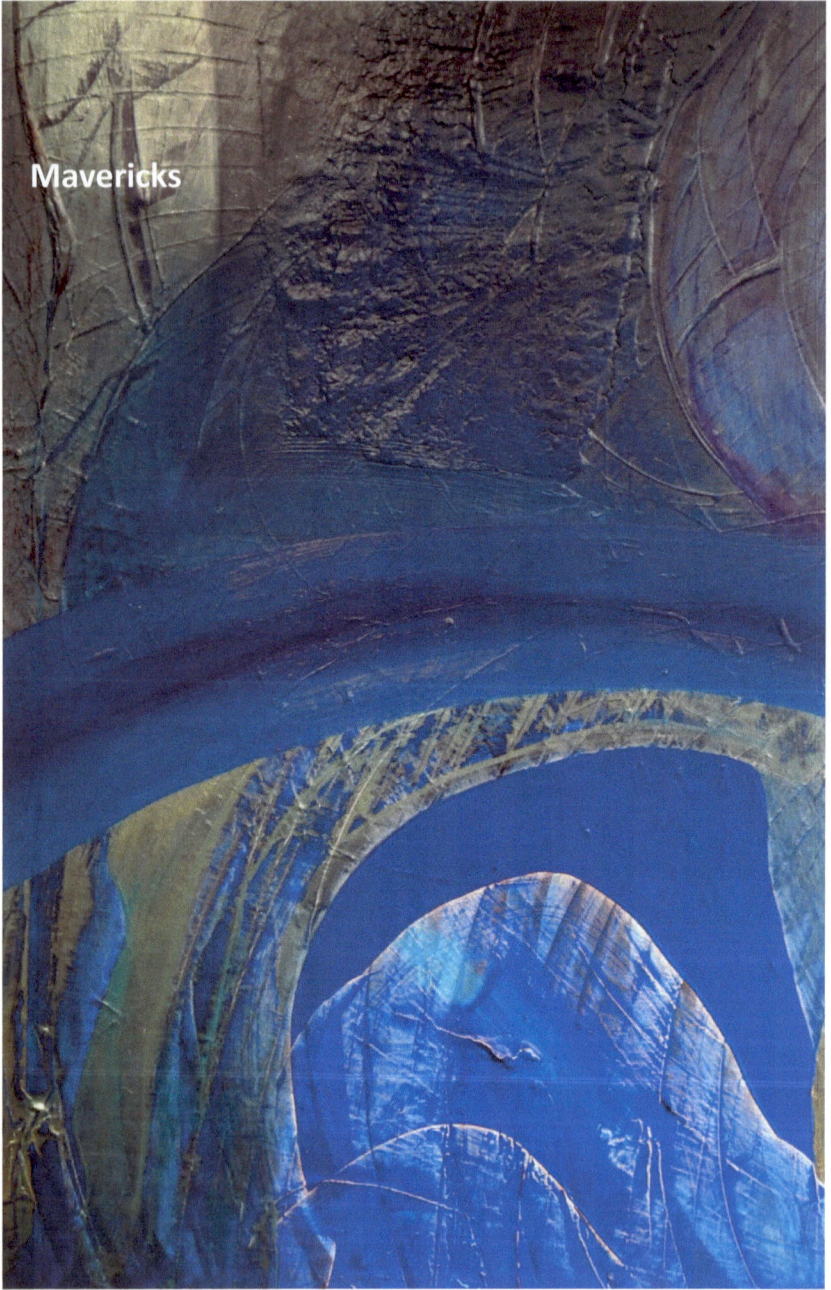

Mavericks

WIPE-OUT
After the painting *Mavericks* by Marco Rosales Shaw
by Sherry Sheehan

On our beach walk, master,
when I escaped you
and leapt leashless into
a tumbling tent of water,
a shock of salt spray
invaded me, and a stray
shark grayed my world
to dark disaster.

In a barking din
my life was undone.
You witnessed
the wipe-out
of my canine self
that was for both of us
a wrenching departure.

Alone, left spent
and stunned,
you can't know
that my soul
has already begun
another lent life.

This time I'll be smaller.
A kitten in welcoming sun,
I've just arrived
as part of a feline litter
whose owner lives inland
on a grand estate
you might appreciate,
even though
it's far from water.

MAVERICKS
After the painting *Mavericks* by Marco Rosales Shaw
by Maria Rosales

Directly behind and immediately beneath the breaking wave,
the steepness of the incline is proportional
to the resulting upthrust.

When a swell passes over a sudden steep slope,
the force of the upthrust
causes the top of the wave to be thrown
forward,
forming a curtain of water which plunges
to the trough below.

The body speaks first.
Then the fear.

Prepare for flight.
Imagine the plunge.
Brace for impact.

Loving him has been like that.

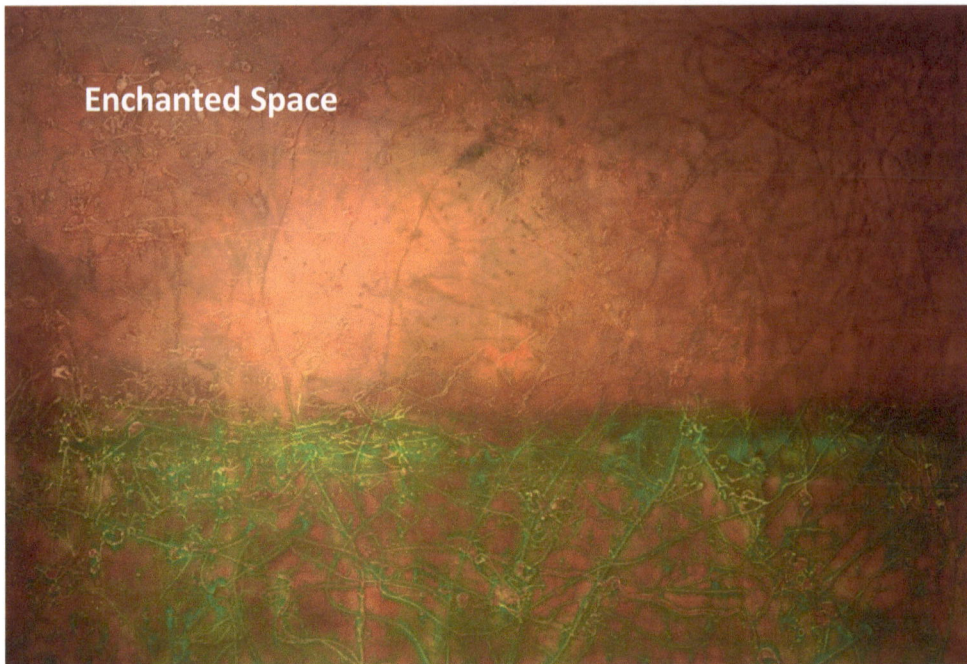
Enchanted Space

THE SPACE BETWEEN
After the painting *Enchanted Space* by Marco Rosales Shaw
by Susan Condeff

The space between you and me
Is vivid
Connected
By memories of bodies entwined
Sound and sight
Verbal and non-verbal
By darkness and light

I am red like desire
You are green like young and wild

The space between you and me
Enchanted.

The space between you and me
Grows murky
Connected
By loss, disappointment and time
Your green has crossed the line
Now green and red combined

The space between you and me
Engraved

The space between you and me
Became mud
Connected
By hurt, damage and pain

My red became blood
Your green became black rain
The space between you and me
Entombed

About the Poets

Suzanne Bruce, born and raised in Oklahoma, holds a B.S. in Education from the University of Tulsa. She did graduate work at Wichita State University in Childhood Behavior Disorders and taught school for over seventeen years. She writes poetry singly as well as does ekphrastic work with local artist Janet Manalo (www.ekphrasticexpressions.com www.ekphrasticalchemy.com). Their book, *Voices Beyond the Canvas* (2007), has been featured in several Bay Area exhibitions. She attended the Napa Valley Writers Conference (2009) and has been selected to write the poetry for the Solano County Women's History Month for the past five years (2010-2014). A member of the Ina Coolbrith Circle, Benicia First Tuesday Poets and the Solano County Library Foundation, she is also active with the Solstice Creative Writers in St. Helena. She reads her poetry at various venues throughout the Napa and Solano counties. Her work has won several poetry prizes and has been published in numerous journals.

Susan Condeff A California native, Susan has lived in the Tri-Valley for many years. She has won several silver medals and honorable mentions at the Alameda County Fair in Poetry. She has been published in the *Las Positas Anthology*, the *Fourth Street Anthology* and the *Tri-Valley Writers 2011 & 2013 Anthology*. She is a member of the California Writers Club—Tri Valley chapter and is now serving as secretary for the club. She is planning to publish her own book of poetry soon. She is also working on several children's books about magical people and places and an adult full length play about love, death and potato chips.

Deborah Fruchey is a native Californian who studied at San Francisco State University. In 1987 her first novel, *The Unwilling Heiress*, was chosen as a Best Book by the American Bookseller's Association. There followed two decades of struggle with mental illness, from which she emerged successfully, publishing a self-help manual on handling mood disorders. *Is There Room for Me, Too? 12 Steps & 12 Strategies for Coping with Mental Illness* has been called "The best book of its kind" by the founder of PeaceLove Foundation, which provides art programs for persons with psychiatric conditions. The book was given a four-star rating by the Clarion Forward Review.

In 2005 Deborah married and moved to Contra Costa County. For three years she hosted an open reading series in Walnut Creek, and for eight years she has published a free poetry newsletter for the greater East Bay area. Her first poetry collection, *Armadilllo*, was published in May by Cyborg Productions. *Armadillo* is the only book Cyborg has released in the last 20 years; shortly thereafter the publisher received an Acker Award for Achievement in the Avant Garde. A review is forthcoming from The Tower Journal.

William Landis: Oberlin College, AB '51, and St. Louis Univ. DDS '56. In 1970, he retired to early poverty to continue painting and poetry. He traveled, stretching the shoestring to reside in Andalusia, Amsterdam, Mykonos, Puerto Vallarta, and rural France.

William has two chapbooks, *Noguchi et al.* and *Takes*. He is winner of the Ad Schuster Annual Citation Grand Prize in `01 and Annual Grand Prize Ina Coolbrith Circle, `09, and has been published in *Runes, Spillway, Pudding House, Riverbabble*, among others. His poetry is often ekphrastic, and he creates many-headed paintings. Willlandis.blogspot.com.

Indigo Moor is a poet, playwright, and author currently residing in Sacramento, CA. His second book of poetry, *Through the Stonecutter's Window*, won Northwestern University Press's *Cave Canem* prize. His first book, *Tap-Root*, was published as part of Main Street Rag's Editor's Select Poetry Series.

Three of his short plays, *Harvest, Shuffling*, and *The Red and Yellow Quartet,* debuted at the 60 Million Plus Theatre's Spring Playwright's festival. His stageplay, *Live! at the Excelsior*, was a finalist for the Images Theatre Playwright Award and is being made into a full-length film.

A graduate of the *Stonecoast MFA Program*—where he studied poetry, fiction, and scriptwriting—Indigo is also a graduate member of the *Artist's Residency Institute* for Teaching Artists and a former Vice President of the *Sacramento Poetry Center.*

Winner of the 2005 *Vesle Fenstermaker Prize for Emerging Writers,* a 2009 Pushcart Prize nominee, and 2008 Jack Kerouac Poetry contest, Indigo's other honors include: finalist finishes for the *T.S. Eliot Prize, Crab Orchard First Book Prize, Saturnalia First Book Award, Naomi Long Madgett Book Award*, and *WordWorks Prize.*

Indigo teaches workshops throughout the Bay Area and the greater Sacramento Valley region.

Stan Morner lives in Walnut Creek, California. A retired high school English teacher with wide-ranging interests, his poetry, essays, travel articles and fiction have appeared in numerous magazines including, 'California English,' 'Kansas Magazine,' 'Clockwatch Review,' 'Anais,' 'An International Journal,' 'Collages and Bricolages,' and 'The San Jose Mercury News.' He has published two chapbooks, *Heartball* and *Pairings*.

Stan's poem, "Mt. Diablo-Naming the Names," won first prize in a poetry contest on poems about Mt. Diablo. He went on to edit the poetry and art book *Mount Diablo 2000. Images.*

As Vice President of the Ina Coolbrith Circle, Stan has worked on two special programs in this capacity. One of these was to help create the Ina Coolbrith Circle Collection in the California State Library. This collection now contains 295 books by members of the organization and about its history and 282 bound copies of the President's Newsletters from 1970-2010. His article "The Ina Coolbrith Collection in the California State Library" appears in *Bulletin*, the publication of the California State Library Foundation. Also, Stan has had a major part in founding *Silver Voices*, a group of performing poets under the auspices of the Ina Coolbrith Circle. *Silver Voices* was established in 2009 with two objectives: 1) to provide poetry programs for seniors and others who do not have access to poetry and 2) to increase interest and membership in the Ina Coolbrith Circle. Most of their programs are addressed to people in senior centers, assisted living facilities, nursing homes and hospitals.

Maria Rosales' poems have appeared in *Byline, Poetry Depth Quarterly, Poetalk, Meridian, The Dirty Napkin, Benicia Herald, The Contra Costa Times, Nashville Newsletter,* and several anthologies. She has one published chapbook, *Time to Fly* (2001). She was host of the popular poetry series "Poetry at Primo's" in the San Francisco East Bay Area for several years, and has served on the Board of Directors for the Ina Coolbrith Circle since 2007. Maria served as a contributing editor for ARTBEAT, the Arts and Culture Commission of Contra Costa County's online newsletter. Several of her poems have been included in ekphrastic exhibits, and two have been the inspiration for original dance performances by Moving Arts Dance Company.

Sherry Sheehan, born and raised in Hawaii, was a Las Vegas school psychologist before retiring to Crockett. From 2006 through 2010 she was online poet laureate for psoriasis website FlakeHQ.com. Michigan painter Mary Reusch and Sherry published *PoArtry*. With former Bay Area artist Robert Chapla she published *Across Currents*. She has participated in ekphrastic exhibits in Benicia, Crockett, Danville, Fairfield, Livermore, Martinez, and Rush Ranch in California, as well as in Indiana and Michigan. Sherry's poems are in all five anthologies of the Benicia First Tuesday Poets, all five issues of *Carquinez Poetry Review*, and the last five Ina Coolbrith Circle *Gatherings*.

Deborah Silverman was born and raised in Washington, D. C. Majoring in philosophy in college and graduate school, she received master's degrees in philosophy and in science, and a doctoral degree in psychology from UCSF. She is now retired from her private practice as a psychologist and as an associate clinical professor. She has been privileged to live in a wide variety of places in the United States and to travel broadly and deeply, including living two years in Thailand in the '60s. Married to her high school sweetheart 55 years and counting, she and her husband, Merv, are enjoying their three daughters, a son-in-law and a granddaughter, age 15. After 24 years in San Francisco they relocated to Crockett, and she discovered here in the East Bay a love of poetry and poets.

Sandra Lee Stillwell is the author of *In a Dress Made of Butterflies* published by Poetic Matrix Press. She has won many awards and is widely published. She resides in Lake County and is active in both the poetry scene and the arts community. She has found both communities welcoming and recently read with both Casey Carney and James Blue Wolf, present and past laureates of Lake County.

After the poetry reading, Campbell Theatre, October 25, 2014,
by Michael Paster

I had not heard of that word before, ekphrasis - and now you have given me an experience of what this means. The chemistry, alchemy, and biology, the snythesis and botany, the larger meaning that is created when a process is publicly shared in a magical space like this little theater.

> *poetry.....wonder, wounded... pain and suffering, delay, anxiety, waiting, pleasure, emotions, and...*

> *Icarus - a red, orange, amalgamation and fusion of energy, filled with imagery. emotion*

> *(Sueño en el Tropico) Primordial - greens, whites and yellow, within a linear vertical net of some other space and time, fog, misty moisture, 120,000,000 years ago*

> *Mavericks - inside a gigantic wave, somehow peaceful, safe. Layers of blues, whites above and below, motion.*

> *Beckoning....*

Editor's note: Michael stepped up to the microphone during the open reading after the October 25th program, and made the above stream-of-consciousness comments. Michael is a visual artist, not a poet, and he was not presenting a poem – but his reaction to the presentation of poetry and art catapulted him to the stage. The passion and emotion in his voice moved me to tears. Thank you, Michael, for the gift of that moment.

Maria Rosales

www.ingramcontent.com/pod-product-compliance
Lightning Source LLC
Chambersburg PA
CBHW041758040426
42447CB00001B/14